HELLISH RELISH

HELLISH RELISH

*Sizzling Salsas and Devilish Dips from
the Kitchens of New Mexico*

SHARON NIEDERMAN

Photography by
EDUARDO FUSS

HarperCollinsWest
A Division of HarperCollinsPublishers

Hellish Relish
Library of Congress Cataloging-in-Publication Data

Niederman, Sharon.
Hellish Relish: Sizzling Salsas and Devilish Dips from
the Kitchens of New Mexico / Sharon Niederman;
with photographs by Eduardo Fuss — 1st ed.

Design: Ingalls + Associates
Designers: Tom Ingalls and Rebekah Lee

p. cm.
Includes index.
ISBN 0-06-258539-8 : $16.00
1. Salsa (Cookery) 2. Dips (Appetizers) 3. Cookery—New Mexico.
I. Title.
TX819.S29N54 1994
641.8'12—dc20   93-41280 CIP

Printed in Singapore

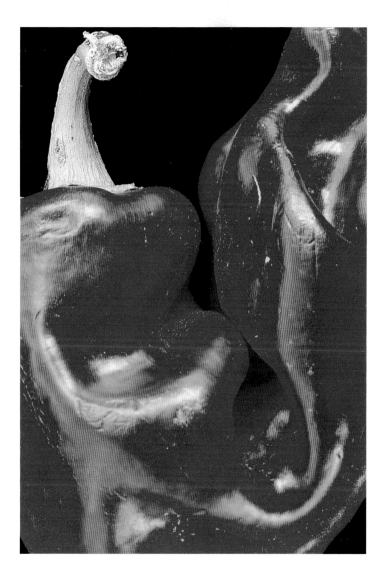

Contents

Introduction

Recipes

Resources

INTRODUCTION

In addition to Spanish, English, Tiwa, Tewa and Towa, another language is spoken in New Mexico—the language of Chile. Walk into any cafe, gas station or grocery store from Questa to Las Cruces, start talking Chile, and you're sure to have yourself a conversation. And it's easy to pick up the fundamentals. An appreciation of the colorful, spicy peppers, the places where they are grown and the people who grow them will give you initial fluency. Toss in some knowledge of recipes, the willingness to travel anywhere to seek out the best, and a strong opinion or two on your preferences for red or green, and you'll soon be able to keep up with the natives.

Chile connoisseurship is essential to the identity of every New Mexican. The comment, "He (or she) really knows his chile" is considered a high compliment. And chile knows no social boundaries. Young or old, rich or poor, male or female, old-timer or newcomer, chile is an equal opportunity experience. No self-respecting New Mexican is ever likely to admit in public that he or she dislikes chile. While such a confession may not be grounds for revoking your citizenship, it will certainly elicit strange looks.

Only in New Mexico, at the end of the Santa Fe Trail, where Indian, pioneer, Mexican, Spanish and other European tastes and customs met and traded with each other in the midst of a long and complicated history, did such a passionate love for the chile pepper take root. And it's that love of chile—its fantastic taste possibilities, its legendary curative powers, and its magical ability to create a sense of well-being—that all New Mexicans share.

We can only speculate whether the first New Mexicans, who arrived some time between 10,000 and 20,000 years ago, brought chile with them, or whether they were drawn here by the promise of unlimited turquoise skies, year-round sunshine and some very special dining

possibilities—perhaps a hot red salsa made from the local wild peppers to spice up an otherwise dreary bison burger.

Here in chile paradise today, everyone waits with anticipation for the chile harvest, when, starting in mid-August, the air is scented with the warm, enticing fragrance of chiles roasting out-of-doors in large wire propane-fired cages. In early fall, around State Fair time, people head for their favorite roadside stand to buy a sack of fresh-roasted green chiles to take home and store in the freezer to use all winter long. Of course, quite a bit finds its way immediately into the chile rellenos, green chile stews, enchiladas and chile salsas we love.

Maybe it's that secure feeling of provisioning, of preparing well for the cold season ahead, that gives us our sense of well-being and makes the trip to buy chile seem like a holiday. And maybe, too, it's that here in New Mexico, we know in our bones that when we eat chile, we're not only eating a magically delicious, nourishing and healing food—we're eating tradition. What sustained the native people for thousands of years, and the Spanish for 500 years here, will sustain us now.

Then, as the season progresses into October, we'll go out and buy our red chile ristra, full, heavy and sweet, and hang it near our front door, a sign of warmth and welcome. It's our way of announcing that we are truly at home, and that we belong to a place we love. It's said the ristra brings good luck—and it certainly is good luck to be able to have the makings of soul-warming red chile salsa right at hand.

Salsa Specialists

Hellish Relish is more than a recipe collection. It's a book about people who really "know their chile", who love it and live it, and who take pride in their ability to grow, select and prepare chile. These New Mexicans have refined their palates through lifetimes of tasting. Like wine connoisseurs after every harvest, they search out the best, their favorite delicacy, whether it's the sweet, red chile sold out of a pickup truck outside the Santuario de Chimayo, or the searingly hot, ancient chile grown at Jemez Pueblo. Their tastes, like their recipes, are highly personal.

The cooks featured here are the chile artists, and their kitchens are their studios, where they create beauty in the form of a ruby-jeweled bowl of rich red salsa or a pungent, garlicky dish of roasted green salsa to spark the appetite. Like all true art work, the salsas they serve are made by hand, carefully, from only the very best raw materials, and mixed with a good measure of each creator's individuality.

These salsa specialists know that when you bring out the salsa, you bring out the fun and the friendship. A great bowl of salsa is a gathering point: around it, talk and laughter are bound to flow. Serving salsa is a simple way of entertaining that makes people feel comfortable and at home. Eating salsa is an immediate way of experiencing the flavor and vibrancy of the chile.

Even better than putting one bowl of salsa on the table, see what happens when you serve several salsas at once, say, a chile con queso with a tomatillo-jalapeño, a guacamole and a good fresh red. It's possible to please the fire-eater and those with timid tastebuds, while giving your guests the opportunity to sample new salsas.

Kitchen Fables and Folklore

Like the tremendous variety of people and places that make New Mexico so special, the kitchens where this salsa magic is made span a great variety of styles: from the open mesquite grill of a bustling, posh Santa Fe restaurant to a plain, white room on a sunny side street in Hatch; from a campfire above Abiquiu to a rehabilitated downtown Albuquerque Victorian; and from a woodstove in a handmade adobe to a historic Tesuque estate. *Hellish Relish* brings you along the backroads into these kitchens up and down the state, to share the treasured, private recipes of people from the heart of New Mexico.

The search for these kitchens requires a pilgrimage. Once outside city limits, most homes do not have simple addresses. People here still go by landmarks when they give directions: take the paved road until you get to the "dip" sign, go left, turn right after the arroyo, go up the hill to the big cottonwood, take the fifth dirt road and look for the

blue mailbox. Having reached your destination without getting seriously lost, you are happy to sit across from your host at the kitchen table, while he or she prepares a treasured recipe. This encounter offers a special intimacy, for mixed in with the hand-chopped ingredients are memories, tales, reminiscences, confidences and priceless tips.

In these pages you will find kitchen fables and folklore as well as cooking instructions, given generously by all who contributed. Most of these recipes are so much the personal creation of the cooks that their measurements had never been previously recorded—it was always just "a pinch of this" and "a handful of that."

Advice to the Cook

Hellish Relish offers recipes to please those who were born with scorchproof tastebuds as well as those who prefer medium to mild. You can adjust many of the recipes to make them more or less hot. You may start out preferring milder dishes, then, like many people, find your craving for hotter sensation increases. In that case, you can add another jalapeño or move on to the hotter recipes included here.

Chiles are unpredictable. Each batch is unique. Even the same variety of chile varies in taste from season to season, depending on growing conditions. Therefore, it is important to taste as you go. And remember: chile is a very personal experience. Feel free to experiment and alter any recipe to suit your own taste. Remember, too, that the longer a salsa sits in your refrigerator, the hotter it gets. One teaspoon of red chile today may taste like you spilled the chile jar tomorrow.

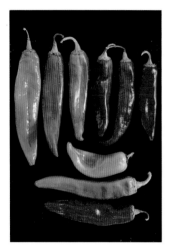

There are two kinds of people in the world—those who love cilantro and those who detest the herb. In most cases, the cilantro in these recipes is optional. Spices that go especially well with chile are garlic, cumin and oregano, and these may generally be added to any recipe.

Just as New Mexicans put up a batch of chile in the fall to last through the winter, you can prepare enough frozen chile while it is in season to keep you warm for many months. Chile comes in many forms: powders, both coarse and fine: dried red, the pods bagged or in ristras; fresh; frozen and canned. Fresh is by far the best, of course, but your own frozen makes an excellent second. You will find that New Mexico's kitchen wizards are not particularly shy about opening a can from time to time. The ingredients in these recipes are now accessible in most supermarkets. And while many salsas call for Chimayo chile— the ingredient of choice in New Mexico—if you cannot obtain Chimayo, you may substitute a good, finely-ground red chile instead.

Chile Preparation

The way to choose your chile is similar to the way you customarily select fruit. Look for chile that is smooth, symmetrical, bright green, crisp and feels firm when squeezed. Avoid chile with bruises, soft spots, shriveled skin or misshapen pods. Chile that is "meaty" will be milder.

When choosing red chile, look for a uniform dark red color, as the lighter, more orange-toned chile powders tend to have seed and stem ground in, making the taste bitter. Avoid chile powder that has other spices, such as oregano or cumin, blended in. Insist on pure chile.

When working with chile, always wear rubber gloves. Keep your hands away from your eyes and face. Capsaicin, the chemical responsible for the chile's heat, can bite you.

In preparing your green chile, the goal is to blister each chile skin as evenly as possible, so the skin can be peeled. First, wash and dry your chiles. Then, make a small slit in the side to allow steam to escape. Use one of three heat sources: a charcoal grill; a broiler set at 400-450°F; or a gas or electric range top covered with a piece of wire mesh. Place the chiles near the heat source (4-6 inches if using a grill or broiler), turning frequently. This roasting process should take 6-8 minutes.

Remove the chiles from the heat, placing them immediately in a brown paper bag or plastic bag, or cover them with a damp towel for 15 minutes to continue the steaming process. If you are using them right away, you will be able to peel them. If not, you can wrap them in plastic or aluminum foil and store them in the freezer. It's easier to peel chiles that have been frozen, so peel and seed them as you need them.

The traditional Indian way of preparing green chile is to simply roast, peel and mash the chiles, adding very little seasoning, maybe just some garlic. This green chile pulp is then added to a stew of meat, potatoes and tomato. Indians traditionally did not use very much salsa—it was introduced as part of the Spanish and Mexican influence. However, salsa has made its way into the Indian diet of today.

For a basic red chile sauce, take a half-dozen or so dried red pods, or snip them from your ristra. If you take them from the top, your ristra will retain its shape. Toast them very carefully in a 250°F oven, with the door open, for a minute or two, just until fragrant. Pour boiling water over the toasted pods, and let them stand for a half-hour. Remove the stems and seeds, place the pods in a blender with a bit of the soaking water, blend and strain. Add garlic, cumin, oregano and salt to taste. You can take this process one step further by simmering the red sauce on very low heat for 15-20 minutes. You now have a basic red sauce to use in salsas or over enchiladas, burritos, eggs or whatever you please.

For fresh red chile powder, simply toss a few toasted pods in the blender and press "grind."

Chile Care

The best way to care for your chile powders is to treat them like good coffee. Store them in air-tight bags and keep them in the freezer, refrigerator or other cool, dark place. You may want to keep a small amount out in a salt shaker on the table. Keep chile out of the light and away from your stove. You may want to keep your ristra in your kitchen to use as needed, or you may decide to take it apart and freeze the peppers, especially if you live in a humid climate where chile is prone to mildew. Eventually light will damage your ristra: as it loses color, it loses flavor. So, unless you're planning to keep your ristra purely decorative, you'll want to use it before you lose it.

Chile Anatomy

The chile gets its heat from the supposedly addictive substance, capsaicin, found in the heart and membrane of the pepper. Contrary to popular belief, the seeds themselves are not hot, but they taste hot because they absorb so much capsaicin. Chile heat depends on a number of factors—first of all, the chile variety, but also on growing location, time of year harvested, climate and amount of moisture in any given growing season.

Red chile is simply green chile in its ripened, mature stage. Green chile left in the field will naturally turn red.

A member of the solanaceae or nightshade family, chile is closely related to the tomato, potato, eggplant and tobacco plants. The precise botanical definition of chile remains a source of confusion. Some consider the peppers as vegetables but, technically, they are berries. When chile is dried, it is considered a spice.

Chile Varieties

The recipes in *Hellish Relish* depend on chiles grown in New Mexico. They are also grown in quantities in California, Arizona and Mexico. When you buy chile labeled "Hatch," you are purchasing the commercially-developed type known as New Mexico 6-10 chile, and the Big Jim, popular for rellenos and growing in home gardens, which offers a middle-range heat.

When it comes to red chile grown in the high mountain villages of Chimayo and Dixon, Velarde and Peñasco are the finest. These chiles are descended from ancient stock, cultivated in small batches, and fed by water from community acequias (ditches) that flows from the Rio Grande, Chama and Embudo rivers. Each variety has its special inflections, so enjoy yourself by tasting and experimenting to discover your favorites. You can't go wrong with red Chimayo chile.

Other chile varieties grown in New Mexico include: jalapeño, de arbol, cayenne, pasilla, habanero and pequin. The habanero is said to be the hottest of them all—at least 100 times hotter than the jalapeño! The tiny pequin, resembling the de arbol, packs quite a heat punch and is a favorite of many old-timers. The jalapeño has an easily recognizable flavor that blends well with other green chiles. In its smoked state, sold dry or canned and packed in adobo sauce, it's known as the chipotle, currently a popular favorite and used widely in the "New Southwest" cooking you are likely to encounter in many upscale Santa Fe restaurants. The large, mild poblano from Mexico, when smoked, is known as the ancho, an essential ingredient of mole sauces. The serrano is often served pickled.

Chile Roots

The word "chile" is a Spanish spelling of the Aztec, or Nahuatl, word for pepper. What we call chile originated in South America, in the area that is now Brazil and Bolivia, and was spread by birds through the continent and northward. Chile was cultivated extensively by the Incas and later by Mayans, Toltecs and Aztecs, who grew dozens of varieties. While the standard historical line maintains that the Spanish brought chiles to New Mexico and introduced them to the Pueblo Indians at the time of the conquest, Indian belief has it that chiles were grown in New Mexico centuries prior to the arrival of the Spanish. While it is possible that wild chiles grew in New Mexico, it is also highly possible that they were introduced early on through trade with the ancient tribes of Mexico and South America. And while chiles are not part of the religious beliefs of Indians, as is corn, chile dishes are customarily eaten three times a day, and red and green chiles are served at all feasts and ceremonies.

Along with corn, beans and squash, chile is one of the four basic, original foods of the native people of the western hemisphere. That means that people have been eating chile here for 10,000 years.

After the Spanish, starting with Columbus, discovered and fell in love with chile, the spice began a round-the-world cuisine revolution. Following trade routes, the chile voyaged from Spain and Portugal into Italy. The Turks of the Ottoman Empire brought paprika and chiles to Hungary and North America. Chiles arrived in India on board Portuguese trading ships. From there, they made their way to Nepal, Tibet and China, transforming cuisine along the way.

Chile Power

Colorful lore surrounds the chile pepper. It's long been believed to have power as an aphrodisiac, as well as a pain-killer, a cure for coughs and sore throats and a guardian against evil spirits. Of special interest today is the chile's excellent nutritional value. High in vitamins A and C, packed with betacarotene, the low-calorie chile is also low in cholesterol, making it a culinary darling for our day. Here in New Mexico, the chile's ability to relieve coughs and cold symptoms is taken quite seriously, and it is commonly used as a poultice to relieve chronic pain. Initially, tiny amounts of chopped seeds and capsaicin-loaded membrane are placed on an arthritic joint, then increased as tolerance increases.

Chile derives much of its reputation as a pain-killer and bringer of well-being from the actual chemical effect its burning capsaicin has on the brain. When you eat—or touch—chile, the skin sends a pain signal to the brain, setting off a release of endorphins, those honored hormones of pleasure. The more, and the hotter, chiles you consume, the greater the endorphin payoff. The result: serious chile addiction.

But how do you know when you qualify as a true chile addict? If you haven't had your chile fix in a day or two and find yourself craving the stuff, it's too late. You're hooked, and you are in real danger of becoming depressed if deprived. Most of the population of New Mexico is certifiably chile-addicted, obsessed with finding the best, discovering the most delicious ways of fixing it, and willing to drive long distances in search of the next great chile-eating experience.

Whether you are a chile novice, chile dabbler or full-fledged chile addict, you will enjoy these authentic salsa recipes from the kitchens of the world's greatest chile lovers.

Sharon Niederman

FARMER'S MARKET SALSA

Stanley and Rose Mary Crawford

From the earliest summer that brings forth fresh, tender greens, through the long, golden fall yielding its pumpkins, blue corn and apples, the Santa Fe Farmer's Market is the town's most beloved and lively event. And amidst the plenty—the flowers, the melons, the exquisite baby vegetables, the music and the delicious baked goods, homemade jams and pestos—Stan and Rose Mary Crawford can be found selling their garlic, carrots, sweet onions and dried flowers.

They make the drive into town from the little village of Dixon to the south of Taos, now inhabited by the descendents of ancient Hispanic families, artists and craftspeople. There, in the adobe home they built themselves, the Crawfords share a life of writing, organic farming and rich community; a life Stan, who also serves as president of the Farmer's Market, has written about so eloquently in books such as *Mayordomo* and *A Garlic Testament*.

In addition to her involvement with the annual fall Dixon Studio Tour, when local artisans open their studios to visitors, Rose Mary is busy all summer canning and drying the abundance of their few acres.

She prepares this joyous-tasting salsa from the home grown vegetables she and Stan bring to the Farmer's Market. It features a combination of both fresh and roasted green chiles, and it is absolutely sensational. While Rose Mary says this will keep better than a week—in her house, "it doesn't keep two hours!"

Farmer's Market Salsa

1 blenderful nice, ripe garden tomatoes
1 gorgeous medium sweet onion
3 large cloves of garlic
6 fresh basil leaves
Pinch of oregano
3 mild green chiles, seeded
3 roasted green chiles, seeded and peeled
Pinch of paprika
1 teaspoon parsley
8-10 drops red wine vinegar
Salt and pepper to taste

Blend tomatoes, onions and chopped garlic with basil. Add oregano, salt and pepper. Boil this mixture 10 minutes, until it thickens. Add and stir chopped fresh green chiles, leaving a few seeds. Cook 5 minutes. Add chopped roasted chiles and paprika. Taste for seasoning. One second before removing from the stove, add finely chopped parsley and wine vinegar. Yields "three small margarine containers of salsa."

Grandmother Sadie's Pot La Gel

Diana Bryer

Artist Diana Bryer draws her inspiration from traditional Hispanic and Native American customs she observes in and around the village of Santa Cruz where she lives. Her soulful images of ristra makers have the same rich colors as folk artists' retablos: her fanciful renditions of people dancing, hawks soaring, horses galloping and angels hovering above the mesas bring us into a dreamy New Mexico landscape of magic and myth.

This Los Angeles native has been remodeling her adobe house and studio, with its red tin roof since 1979, when she moved in. "I want a Frida Kahlo kitchen," she says, expanding on plans she has to paint the vigas (beams) with intricate designs. Frida would approve of this kitchen, filled with papier-mache parrots, odd pieces of Victorian silver and mismatched Blue Willow and hand-painted china, with bundles of herbs hung from the ceiling to dry.

She grinds her spices in the pig-faced granite metate that belonged to her husband Rudy's aunt; and she still makes fresh tortillas on the cast-iron comal he brought her when they were courting. "I may be one of the last women around Española who still makes her own tortillas," she says, "but I like to come into the kitchen early in the morning and do that."

Her pride and joy is her six-burner, double-oven vintage O'Keefe & Merritt stove, the heart of her kitchen. "My mother had one, and I had to have one, too," she says. "It's my Cadillac, and I couldn't cook without it. I looked for years until I found it."

Her Grandmother Sadie's Pot La Gel is one of her favorite recipes, and she prepares this eggplant relish in her grandmother's well-worn wooden bowl, now used only for this purpose. She adds red chile to what she terms "the national Jewish dish of Romania. All the Bryer family makes this. It's sentimental and I love it. When I make it, it feels like I'm at home again."

Grandmother Sadie's Pot La Gel

Three eggplants (elongated
    rather than round)
I bell pepper, chopped
I sweet red pepper, chopped
2-3 scallions, chopped
I teaspoon dry basil leaves
I teaspoon dry oregano leaves
I garlic clove, run through a garlic press

I tablespoon olive oil
2 tablespoons red wine vinegar
I teaspoon coarse-ground red chile

Roast the eggplants by placing them directly on the burners, on a high gas flame (preferred method) or under the broiler. When they turn black on one side (about five minutes), turn them. Let them cool ½ hour. Remove stems. Cut them in half with a sharp knife, and gently scrape the pulp into a non-metal bowl. (Try to keep the charred skin out, but don't mind if a few bits get in.) Add the other ingredients, one by one. Take a hand chopper with a blade and chop finely for about 10 minutes, turning the bowl as you go. (Diana insists that this dish must be chopped by hand.) When it is all well mixed, but still of a firm consistency, chill for 1 hour in the refrigerator.

This eggplant relish is traditionally served with challah, but Diana serves it on her homemade tortillas, or with crackers, or as part of an appetizer platter with green and ripe olives, raw vegetables, hard-boiled eggs and cheeses. She recommends it as well as a relish for pot roast.

Rojo Rico Salsa

Ralph Sena

Silversmith Ralph Sena crafts his Rojo Rico salsa the way he fashions his gleaming silver heartline bears—with the attention and patience that allow the basic ingredients to reveal their fullest beauty. The confidence he carries in his hands prevails as he works in the compact, bright kitchen of the snug Chimayo house he built himself, just as it does in his saddle-making. While his bears, some with touches of gold, others with turquoise inlay, travel to Goldwater's, Neiman-Marcus and the galleries and museums of Taos and Santa Fe, his rich red chile salsa is happily consumed at home every day by friends and family, which includes the three grown daughters he raised himself.

An avid outdoorsman, Ralph has a lifelong fascination with the spirit of the bear. "It stands for motherhood, strength, nurturing and it is a guardian. I like those qualities," he says. He lifts the lid of the Dutch oven simmering on the stove to check the chicken marinated in Rojo Rico, allowing a a burst of fragrant steam to scent the kitchen. His mother's wood stove occupies the place of honor here. "I've been making palitos (kindling) for this stove since I was as tall as the ax handle," he laughs.

Ralph serves his Rojo Rico in a heavy, handmade pottery bowl, its subdued gray and blue setting off the shimmering deep scarlet of the salsa. The thick, luxurious mixture blazes in the bowl, a hot fire on a rainy November night. The taste of the salsa ripples out, from the first perfume to the lingering slow burn at the end.

And the chile he uses is "chile del pais," the local Chimayo chile, grown from seeds saved over generations. This Chimayo chile, he explains, is smaller, the meat is thinner and it's "rinde mas," which means it "gives more." "I played with this recipe," he says. "I wanted texture, and I wanted flavor."

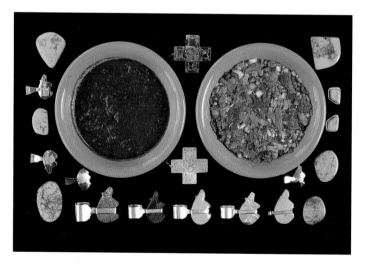

Rojo Rico

½ cup caribe (coarse ground red
    chile with seeds)
2 heaping tablespoons polvo
    (powdered red chile)
1 cup boiling water
12 red chile pods
4 cloves garlic
¼ teaspoon cumin
½ teaspoon oregano
salt to taste

To the caribe and polvo, add the cup
boiling water and let stand. Clean, seed
and stem the chile pods, then rehydrate
by steeping them in boiling water until
the meat "revives" (approximately 15
minutes). Combine the rehydrated chile
pods with the garlic in the blender. To
this mixture, add the cumin and
oregano. Add the blended chiles to the
caribe and polvo mixture. Serve with
blue corn chips.

ROASTED TOMATO-DE ARBOL SALSA

Cheryl Snyder - Old Mexico Grill

D ining at the Old Mexico Grill is as close as you can get to eating in Mexico City, without ever leaving Santa Fe. When locals get tired of traditional New Mexican cooking—and they do—they come to the Old Mexico Grill to refresh their palates with the moles, poblanos en nogada and other distinctly Mexican dishes. Located in an inconspicuous corner of an everyday shopping center, the restaurant seems like a surprise discovery, with its comfortable, open dining area built around a large central pecan wood-fired grill. Here appreciative diners can observe the preparation of their sizzling fajitas al carbon, amidst the leaping flames. The cuisine here is not based on New Mexico red or green chile; rather, it is flavored with spicy combinations of imported peppers—anchos, mulattos, cascabels, pasillas and chipotles.

For sous-chef/pastry chef Cheryl Snyder, the road to the Old Mexico Grill from her home in Shamrock, Texas, where she grew up eating a cross between Southern and Pennsylvania Dutch food, was paved with stops at cooking school La Varenne and in Veracruz with Diana Kennedy. "The food we serve is not Spanish, and it is not Southwestern," says Cheryl. "The origins of this food are with the Mayan, Aztec and Toltec people: we serve the authentic regional food of Mexico, with an emphasis on the Yucatan."

In Mexico, she says, the chiles are always toasted, lightly, on the comal, the long iron griddle used primarily for warming tortillas. Toasting them, which can be done in a cast iron skillet, brings out the oil and carmelizes the natural sugars to sweeten them.

Roasted Tomato-de Arbol Salsa is typical of the Old Mexico Grill's spin on Mexican cooking. And the more you eat, the more you want.

Roasted Tomato-de Arbol Salsa

¾ ounce de Arbol chile
I and ½ to 2 pounds fresh
    tomatoes (use half romas)
3 garlic cloves
I-14½ ounce can tomatoes
¼ tablespoon salt
Enough oil to toast the chile

Stem and seed the de Arbol chile. Toast it in oil, just until fragrant, watching very carefully so it does not burn and turn bitter. Roast the fresh tomatoes on a grill or under a broiler until the skins turn black. Place them, charred skins and all, in the blender with diced canned tomatoes, roasted chile, garlic and salt. Blend until smooth. Makes one quart salsa. You can substitute pequin or serrano for the de Arbol chile.

BLACK BEAN-POBLANO SALSA

Jill Momaday

Brilliant color is a key attraction of Santa Fe actress and model Jill Momaday's Black Bean-Poblano Salsa. The combination of brilliant red, green and yellow peppers interplayed with the dark chocolate-colored black beans is as irresistible to a guest as a hot pink hibiscus is to a hummingbird. Once drawn to this colorful display, the avid muncher will discover subtle yet distinct layers of warm spice, as red chile laces with savory poblano.

"I love color," Jill says, "and I love to see a plate of food that pleases you aesthetically." She favors wooden bowls and utensils for their smooth feel, heft and solidity; her use of wooden serving bowls echoes her taste for simple fare prepared with fresh vegetables.

"I love to be adventurous with my chiles," she says. "Being in New Mexico means we have such wonderful indigenous foods to work with. New Mexico cuisine always has room for innovation. We draw from the original foods, but we can always take them so much further.

"One of my favorite things in the world to do is to pack a bowl of this salsa with two or three good cheeses, a bottle of wine, a dear friend and my dog, Bella, and take off the day for a picnic in the mountains."

After modeling in New York and Paris, Jill played in the *Lucky Luke* television series; recently, she appeared with Sam Shepard in *Silent Tongue* and acted in a run of *Black Elk Speaks*. She now lives in the house off Canyon Road in Santa Fe where she grew up. Here she can sit in her backyard with a view of the mountains and enjoy the fresh delicate scent of sage and juniper wafting through on an early summer evening—the perfect time to serve Black Bean-Poblano Salsa to a few friends who've dropped by.

Black Bean-Poblano Salsa

2 cans black beans
¼ cup red onion, minced
1 clove garlic, minced
2 tablespoons Chimayo red chile, finely ground
½ teaspoon ground cumin
½ cup fresh cilantro, chopped (optional)
½ cup green pepper, diced
½ cup red pepper, diced
½ cup yellow pepper, diced
1 poblano, minced
Juice of 3-4 fresh-squeezed limes

Drain the black beans and wash them. Mix all ingredients, adding the lime juice last. Refrigerate at least an hour. If desired, top with two or three tablespoons of creme fraiche or sour cream and decorate with sprigs of fresh parsley.

MEDITERRANEAN SALSA

Nancy Gerlach

The combination of black olives and parsley gives this salsa a taste of Provence—a taste that brings fond associations to chile maven Nancy Gerlach. *Chile Pepper* magazine's food editor, Nancy recalls that when she and her husband, Jeff, were first married, they "sold everything" and traveled in Europe for a year and a half. "We spent a lot of time around the Mediterranean, and this salsa is reminiscent of the great food we had."

Even as a child growing up in Long Beach, California, Nancy always liked hot foods. A chile pioneer who's been writing about the hot subject of peppers since 1978, today Nancy and her husband share a "chile lifestyle." "We sell it, we eat it, we grow it and I write about it," this clear-eyed, happy-looking woman laughs. Living in a semi-rural neighborhood, alongside the Rio Grande, the Gerlachs grow more than 40 kinds of chile in their enormous garden.

Nancy's compact kitchen, where she develops and tests dozens of chile recipes, features crowded carousels of spices, vinegars, oils and sauces, all in easy reach on open shelves, all begging to be used and mixed together in new and unique ways. "I collect habanero hot sauces," she says of her treasured assortment, gathered on trips to the Yucatan and the Caribbean. The Gerlachs' mail order chile business, Old Southwest Trading Company, gives them an excuse to travel—"to hunt for new products."

Hanging baskets, a row of excellent knives on a wall rack, orange enamel cookware affixed to the side of a cabinet stocked with blue-and-white hand-pointed dinnerware, all make for a kitchen that creatively utilizes every inch of space. Ceramic chile ristras, straw animals and brightly-colored tin-and-mirror ornaments decorate every nook. This kitchen beckons to the cook who just loves to have fun.

This recipe goes especially well with grilled fish. Or, you might like to try it as a relish on tuna, turkey or cheese sandwiches.

Mediterranean Salsa

1 tablespoon crushed dried red New
   Mexican chile, seeds included
1 6-ounce can black olives, chopped
2 tablespoons olive oil
2 tablespoons white vinegar

1 tablespoons chopped parsley
   (preferably Italian)
1 tablespoon capers
⅛ teaspoon sugar

Combine all ingredients and allow to sit a couple of hours before serving. Yields 2 cups.

SIZZLING SALSA

Susan Hazen-Hammond

Writer Susan Hazen-Hammond's Sizzling Salsa is a celebration of her love of the serrano pepper. "I love the taste of the serrano," she says. "I like it for its sudden heat and quiet fade. Taste it," she says, "and a bullet of heat will pass through you." When it's gone, the sensation of that pepper "lures you on for the next hit."

In her cozy Santa Fe kitchen, Susan likes nothing better than to prepare a variety of salsas, which she loves to give as gifts. "The reason I like chiles to begin with is because they help us feel connected with ourselves and others. A real salsa wakes you up, makes you feel alive, and puts you in touch with your senses," she says. She loves making salsa, because to her, "it's not just a food. I'm not just putting ingredients together. I'm creating an event, something people will enjoy together; a great social connection."

When Susan and her husband, Eduardo Fuss, entertain at intimate, informal dinner parties (usually no more than two guests), she will usually serve two salsas: one with heat and one without. "I like to serve salsas in black dishes," she says, "because the red stands out so well on them."

Sizzling Salsa

2 small or one large tomato
9 green serrano or serranito peppers
1 small or ½ large red bell pepper
½ medium onion
6 stalks cilantro
2 cloves garlic
½ cup water
2 tablespoons red wine vinegar
2 tablespoons canola or corn oil
½ teaspoon salt

Cut the tomatoes in fourths. Wearing rubber gloves, remove and discard the stems of the serrano peppers, then cut in halves. Cut the red bell and onion in fourths.

Remove the leaves from the cilantro stalks and discard the stalks. Place the tomatoes, serranos, bell pepper, onion, cilantro leaves and garlic in the blender. Add water and vinegar and chop at medium speed just until the mixture in reduced to small chunks. Add oil to a stainless steel skillet and pour the salsa mixture in. Add salt. Bring to a low boil. Continue to cook at a low boil for four or five minutes, stirring frequently. Cool and store in a covered jar in the refrigerator.

For a milder salsa, reduce the number of peppers. For a thicker salsa, reduce the amount of water.

SWEET GREEN CHILE SALSA

Sammie McAdams

On a quiet, sunny side street within shouting distance of the chile fields of Hatch, New Mexico, retired Indian trader Sammie McAdams can be found in her kitchen most days, cooking up a storm. A self-described "main-dish cook" who, despite herself, turns out fresh apple pies, apple cakes and pastelitos (little pastries) that are well-known around town, Sammie started out cooking in big quantities. She grew up on an Ohio dairy farm, and one day when she was eight years old, made five custard pies, one by one, for the farm hands. "My Dad sure bragged on 'em," she recalls. She loves to try new recipes she collects from friends as well as those she cuts out of the paper. Her well-worn cookbooks are stuffed with many years' worth of clippings.

Her completely utilitarian kitchen, lined with immaculate plain white enamel cabinets, looks out on a neat backyard where a red-painted wooden roadrunner goes 'round and 'round in the breeze.

Sammie has been putting up her Sweet Green Chile Salsa for at least 25 years, and she enjoys some just about every day. "I like it chunky," she says. "We usually have a jar open in the refrigerator for anybody that comes along." She likes to put a big spoonful in a bowl of beans. It also goes extremely well with hamburgers, barbeque, broiled chicken, roast pork and other roast meats. "We love it in meatloaf," she says, "and it's not too sweet to eat with chips, either."

Sweet Green Chile Salsa

(Sammie gives this recipe in quantities sufficient for canning. If you want to make a smaller amount , follow those quantities in parentheses.)

1 gallon (1 quart) tomatoes,
   peeled and chopped
½ gallon (2 cups) fresh Hatch green
   chile, mild to medium, chopped
½ gallon (2 cups) onion, diced
1 cup (¼ cup) vinegar

1 (¼) teaspoon cinnamon
1 (¼) teaspoon allspice
2 (½) heaping tablespoons red
   chile powder
1 (¼) tablespoon salt

Mix all the ingredients, bring to a boil, cook on low boil until the tomatoes are done and the onions are tender. Cooking time will vary depending on quantities used. Can take from 15-25 minutes. Freezes and keeps very well in the refrigerator.

MINORCAN HELLISH RELISH

Christopher Way

The key ingredient in Hellish Relish is the datil pepper, a fiery devil resembling the habanero and said to be 30 to 100 times hotter than the jalapeño—which certainly qualifies it as one of the big league hots. St. Augustine, Florida, is the home of the datil, where most of them are grown and where, for 300 years, they have been a culinary force to be reckoned with. When, over a decade ago, customers began swiping bottles of his homemade datil hot sauce off the tables of his seafood restaurant, *Barnacle Bill's*, Christopher Way decided to try and meet the public's need. "I figured if people were stealing the sauce, they might pay for it," he says of his motivation for starting his Dat'l Do-It sauce and specialty business.

"Everybody in St. Augustine has a datil plant in their yard," says Chris, "but nobody grows them commercially, so I have to raise my own."

Like the chile peppers of New Mexico, the datils of North Florida have a long and uncertain history. Perhaps they were brought north by tribes of Central America or by early Spanish explorers, or, perhaps they were (as the legend goes) introduced to Florida by the Minorcans, who migrated from the Spanish island of Minorca in the Mediterranean.

Or—as some say—perhaps the datil pepper was introduced to Florida by Spaniards who trekked from Datil, New Mexico, a tiny village on the barren plains of San Augustin, possibly named for a fruit resembling dates said to grow in the nearby Datil Mountains.

Historic speculation aside, Chris Way's Hellish Relish offers a fruit-sweetened blast to toast your tastebuds. If datil peppers aren't available, turn to habaneros, or, if substituting jalapeños, increase the dosage to your taste.

Minorcan Hellish Relish

15 medium pears, peeled and cored
12 bell peppers, mixed red and green
10 onions
8 datil peppers

In a food processor, grind all the above but keep it chunky. Place in a strainer to remove excess juice.

Add the following ingredients to mixture:

1 quart apple cider vinegar
3 cups sugar
3 tablespoons salt
1 tablespoon celery seed
1 tablespoon dry mustard
1 tablespoon tamari

Bring to a boil, reduce to simmer for 20 minutes. Put up in Ball jars.

HOTTER THAN HELL HABANERO SALSA

Susan Hazen-Hammond

Pepper, pepper on the wall, which is the hottest pepper of them all? Habanero, Habanero, Habanero! When it comes to salsa, Santa Fe writer Susan Hazen-Hammond and her husband, photographer Eduardo Fuss (whose photographs grace these pages) definitely like it hot. In fact, Eduardo likes to eat this salsa before bedtime. The vast amount of endorphins it releases give him a "pleasant, warm glow over his tummy."

Inspiration for this salsa came from Susan's son, William, while he was home on a visit from college. When he spotted some fresh habaneros and Tabasco on the kitchen counter one summer morning, he suggested concocting them into a really special salsa. Susan began experimenting. The result: a sleeping potion that's off the Richter scale!

Susan and Eduardo also love to slather generous amounts of this hot, hot, hot salsa on their homemade pizzas. Try it over chile rellenos or burritos, as well as a dip with chips.

Hotter Than Hell Habanero Salsa

1 small tomato
2 medium onions
3 cloves garlic
1 medium red bell pepper
1 fresh habanero pepper
1 fresh Tabasco pepper
1 tablespoon chopped parsley
⅓ cup water
1 tablespoon lemon juice
2 teaspoons canola oil
½ teaspoon salt
½ teaspoon thyme
¼ teaspoon oregano

Cut the tomato, onions, garlic and red bell pepper in fourths. Wearing rubber gloves, remove and discard the stems of the habanero and Tabasco peppers and cut them in half. Place tomato, onion, garlic, all peppers and chopped parsley in the blender. Add water and lemon juice and chop very briefly at medium speed, just until the mixture is reduced to small chunks. Add oil to a stainless steel skillet and pour the salsa mixture in. Add salt, thyme and oregano and stir. Bring to a low boil. Continue to cook at low boil for four or five minutes, stirring frequently. Cool and store in a covered jar in the refrigerator. For a milder salsa, omit the Tabasco pepper. For a thicker salsa, pour off excess juice before storing.

Canned peppers may be substituted for fresh.

JALAPEÑO-TOMATILLO SALSA

Mark Medoff

Having lived in the Las Cruces area for 25 years and taught at New Mexico State University, the author of *Children of a Lesser God*, playwright, screenwriter and novelist Mark Medoff says his roots are so deep in New Mexico that now, "they'd have to dynamite me out. . . . I just love living here. I wasn't born in New Mexico, but I am a New Mexican." And he is one New Mexican who likes his chile hot.

Like many children of the '50s, Mark Medoff was "transfixed by cowboy movies, heroes and Western mythology." Southern New Mexico is the location of several of his plays, including *When You Comin' Back, Red Ryder?* and *Doing a Good One for the Red Man.* He enjoys the semi-rural lifestyle that allows him to look out his windows and have the feeling he's in the country, while his children can walk to school from their five acres on the edge of town. His elegant red-tile-roofed Spanish-style home reveals his fondness for the Southwestern aesthetic, as do his storyteller dolls, primitives and colorful paintings.

He frequently invites film colleagues to Las Cruces, where he prefers to entertain outdoors. At these afternoon get-togethers, he's likely to serve Jalapeño-Tomatillo Salsa.

And, if you've been eyeing those small green tomatoes, called "tomatillos," in their paper husks at the grocery store but haven't known what to do with them, this salsa is a good place to start. Choose ones that are firm, avoiding those with any black spots. Remove the husks gently by running hot water over the tomatillos.

Jalapeño-Tomatillo Salsa

8-12 tomatillos, parboiled, after
    removing husks
4-6 New Mexico chiles, parboiled,
    after removing seeds and pith
1 small onion, chopped
2 garlic cloves, minced
1 teaspoon lime juice or vinegar
1-2 jalapeños, chopped
¼ cup fresh cilantro, chopped (optional)

After peeling and discarding the husks, drop the tomatillos in boiling water for 4 minutes or until they soften slightly. Do the same with the chiles and the jalapeños. Let them each cool. Puree the tomatillos in the blender, then add, one after another, chiles, jalapeños, onion and garlic. Add lime juice or vinegar to taste. If you are a cilantro fan, complete the salsa by blending this herb in as well.

A chopped ripe avocado makes a delicious addition to this salsa, after the blending is complete.

KINGSTON SALSA

Catherine Wanek and Mike Sherlock

When Catherine Wanek and Mike Sherlock set out from Los Angeles in January, 1984, all they wanted was a blissful honeymoon trip through New Mexico. What they ended up with was an historic inn inside the Gila National Forest. The two young film producers fell in love with the abandoned Black Range Lodge in a ghost town named Kingston and, on a whim, they made it theirs.

Since 1988, they've operated the Lodge as a bed and breakfast. The towns of Kingston and nearby Hillsboro have continued since to attract other Hollywood expatriates. The Lodge has been their home and studio, where they continue to write, produce and edit movies. Their annual New Year's Eve potluck is legendary, attracting travelers from Europe and Latin America as well as numerous recognizable film stars—all digging into the enchiladas with gusto.

One side of the big lodge kitchen is outfitted with green vinyl restaurant booths, the kind you can slide into and get lost in for days. Mike jokes that it's a kitchen "you can bowl in." The woodburning stove arrived a century ago in a covered wagon. When you come down for breakfast in the morning, you can help yourself to an assortment of fresh-baked breads and preserves, or fix yourself a couple of eggs. Then you can sit with your coffee and dream about what it was like when the stagecoach stopped here, or chat with the other guests, who may be stopping over on a cross-country bike tour or on their way to Australia. The world passes through this kitchen, but it does so at a leisurely pace, a pace that is in harmony with the spirit of the Lodge.

The intense, capable and good-humored hostess, Catherine, says that whenever she makes her Kingston Salsa, people tell her she should bottle it. "No one can guess the secret ingredient," she says. "It's miso." She recommends it in winter as a favorite boost to the immune system, since it's so heavy on the garlic. If you let it sit in the refrigerator for an hour, the pectin in the chile causes the tomato juice to gel, resulting in a firmly-textured salsa that sits well on a chip. She loves to serve it in a colorful bowl with a mixture of blue and white corn chips.

Kingston Salsa

10 Rio Grande Valley green chiles, hot or mild, to taste; fresh roasted, frozen or re-hydrated, peeled and seeded
8 cloves fresh garlic, or less, to taste
½ bunch cilantro
25 ounces to 1 quart tomato juice, or canned tomatoes
1 tablespoon red miso

Combine all ingredients in blender and puree, about 45 seconds. Refrigerate one hour.

HOLIDAY CRANBERRY SALSA

Carol Glassheim

Carol Glassheim's spice cabinet is as international as her kitchen folk art decor. Indonesian fans adorn the walls and an arrangement of miniature rabbits from China, Hawaii and Mexico, perched around stones found on the beach at Crete compose a table centerpiece. Her well-stocked kitchen shelves contain the useful souvenirs of her travels—colorful, mysterious bottles, jars and cartons of oils, spices and condiments. Her charming, tiny cooking space is living proof that the well-equipped, well-stocked kitchen need not be elaborate.

"My best attribute as a cook is imagination," she says. "That, and an interest in flavors." Consequently, she is not afraid to try new combinations. Inspiration often visits her, bringing her ideas like a sweet potato and red chile casserole or her cranberry salsa with jalapeños. She likes to pair unusual tastes; her green salads often offer surprises in the form of pomegranate seeds, kumquats or strawberries. "I'm not into expense, fuss or careful measurement," she confides. "A great dish doesn't have to be complex."

True to form, she likes to serve her Holiday Cranberry Salsa not only at Thanksgiving and Christmas feasts, but at summer barbeques as well, prepared from cranberries frozen while in season. Whether she brings this sparkling, fruity relish to a potluck or serves it at home, she is always asked for the recipe.

Holiday Cranberry Salsa

1-12 oz. package fresh cranberries
2 whole oranges
½ cup sugar
1 bunch cilantro
½ medium onion
2 jalapeños, de-veined, seeds removed
1 inch chunk fresh ginger root, peeled
¼ teaspoon green chile powder,
    if available

Place cranberries in food processor. Squeeze in the juice of one orange, cut the orange in quarters, and add it, including peel. Peel the other orange, and add it in sections. Add sugar and cilantro. Pulse for 1-2 minutes, until well-blended, while keeping some texture. Slice the onion and jalapeños into the mixture. Add ginger root and process these ingredients with the cranberries. Add green chile powder, to taste, blend. This makes 2-3 cups, keeps very well and can be made a day or two ahead of time. It does get hotter as it sits, however. Wonderful with blue corn chips!

CONFETTI CORN SALSA

Nancy Gerlach

It may not be the chile Bible, but if you swear on a stack of *Chile Pepper* magazines that you love the spicy red and green devils, we'll take your word for it that you're at least on the way toward becoming a true chile addict. Published in Albuquerque, *Chile Pepper: Spicy World Cuisine* has grown steadily. Publisher Robert Spiegel says there are several reasons that explain why chile is so hot: the desire for a healthier diet leads directly to chile as a flavorful substitute for fat and salt; people are more adventurous in their eating; they are traveling more and sampling more exotic cuisines, and, there is a definite addiction factor. Once you're hooked on hot food, you've just got to have it!

From her creations for the pages of *Chile Pepper*, food editor Nancy Gerlach contributes Confetti Corn Salsa. "It goes well with barbeque and looks great on a plate," she says. This eminently eatable salsa is probably as close to Tex-Mex cooking as most New Mexicans are liable to get. Guests are likely to rave over the big bowl of this salsa that Nancy serves at her outdoor summer barbeques, enjoyed in the midst of her huge garden. That's when she likes to test her new recipes out on friends.

As a registered dietician, Nancy made sure that chile got on the menu three times a day at Albuquerque's University Hospital, where she is assistant director of food services. "In New Mexico, chile is a real comfort food," she notes. If chile can comfort the sick, just think what it can do for you when you're feeling well!

Confetti Corn Salsa

5 jalapeño or serrano chiles, stems removed, chopped
1 small bell pepper, stems and seeds removed, diced
1 medium tomato, diced
½ can whole kernel corn
1 small red onion, chopped
1 clove garlic, minced
3 tablespoons olive oil
1 tablespoon lime juice
1 tablespoon finely chopped fresh basil

Combine all the ingredients and allow to sit for a couple of hours before serving. Yields 2 cups. This brightly colored salsa goes well with grilled or barbecued meats and chicken.

PICO REAL SALSA

Ralph Sena

Wearing a baseball cap that says "Del Valle Welding," and moving purposefully from refrigerator to sink to cutting board in his Chimayo kitchen, Ralph Sena is a happy man. Having lived in New Mexico all his life, he is a man who knows his chile, and who knows he knows. It is clear from the seriousness of his tone that this knowledge of chile is a mark of manhood, and as important as other skills essential to living well—hunting, building, riding a horse—in the mountain villages of northern New Mexico. A man has got to know his chiles up here.

The sound of his well-sharpened knife meeting wood, as he slices through onions and peppers, punctuates his conversation. "There's nothing like the real thing," he says, and for his Pico Real (Royal Pico) Ralph insists on the freshest herbs and vegetables. His own variation of pico de gallo (beak of the rooster), the chunky fresh salsa traditionally served with fajitas, is hot, but not too hot, with a current of sweetness running through it. It must be served fresh, for the flavors dim quickly.

His Pico Real recipe makes a substantial amount—approximately 6 cups—but that won't seem like a lot when even a small group of friends gather around. People can't help but eat far more of this salsa than they intend to.

Pico Real

20 large New Mexico green chiles,
    roasted, peeled and seeded, chopped
6 fresh jalapeños, seeded and de-veined,
    diced fine
1 large red onion (Vidalia or Texas
    10-15 are good), diced
6 cloves garlic
½ cup fresh cilantro, chopped
¼ cup fresh oregano, minced
1-#303 can tomatoes or 4 medium
    fresh tomatoes, peeled and diced

Mix all the ingredients except the garlic. Run the garlic through a garlic press and add to the mixture. Salt to taste, if needed.

CAFE SALSA

Alex Martinez, Jr. - Gloria's Place

6:30 a.m., Hatch, New Mexico. One by one, the big pickup trucks pull up outside Gloria's Place. Then, the chile farmers and ranchers, clad in pile-lined denim vests, dusty boots, faded flannel shirts, suspenders and worn jeans, enter the cafe the size of a two-car garage. Each pulls up a chair around the big table at the front, and soon the over-heated room fills with the talk and laughter of men. There's some serious coffee drinking going on here among the men who live, breathe and dream chile each day of their lives. Outside, the big rigs swing past; the faint twang of country music, punctuated by static, plays on the kitchen radio. And just beyond the highway, the chile fields are always waiting, for planting or picking, depending on the season.

If Hatch, New Mexico, holds the title of "Chile Capital of the World," then Gloria's Place is the capital of Hatch. Debbie, the waitress with the friendly smile and the bottomless coffeepot, bustles about, delivering short stacks and plastic squeeze bottles loaded with salsa to heat up eggs over medium. They serve ten gallons a week, easy. "It's so good, you can't stop eating it," says Debbie. "People come here from California, Nevada, Ohio . . . all over. They say it's worth the detour to stop here. That's why we're open seven days a week."

Down south, from Hatch to Mesilla, they boil their jalapeños. As sacrilegious as this practice might seem to northern chile belt dwellers, boiling actually preserves the fresh flavor of the jalapeños while removing some of the burn. Alex Martinez, Jr., proprietor of ten years' standing, invented the recipe for the salsa served at Gloria's Place. It derives its delicious hotness completely from jalapeños. And Debbie is right. Chips were made for this salsa.

Gloria's Place Salsa

12 jalapeños
4 good slices of onion
1 coffee scoop garlic salt
1 small can V-8 juice
2 cans tomatoes

Boil the jalapeños ½ hour. Add them to the blender, skins, seeds and all, with the other ingredients. Add enough canned tomatoes to make 1 blenderful, when combined with the other ingredients. Puree 2-3 minutes.

SUN-DRIED TOMATO SALSA

Rose Mary Crawford

Although she owns shelves of cookbooks, Rose Mary Crawford never uses them to cook with. Instead, she prefers to read them like novels. Dressed in her customary black jeans and black shirt, the tall, fit, energetic Rose Mary dons a Guatemalan vest embroidered with orange and gold flowers as she begins to cook, because, as she says, "I like to have something nice on in the kitchen—and then get a mess all over it. I'm terribly untidy."

Outside this Dixon kitchen window, finches perch on a gourd birdfeeder; geese scatter across the front yard. Sunshine beams across the faded red-painted kitchen table, and excellent fresh-brewed coffee steams from heavy blue-and-white pottery mugs. The biggest influences on Rose Mary's cooking are time spent living in Italy and the continuous harvest of fresh herbs and vegetables she and her husband, Stan, grow on their small garlic farm and, in the winter, produce in their greenhouse. This kitchen, with its garlic braids and dried-flower wreaths, its open handmade cupboards ("we built them 20 years ago and were going to put doors on them but never did"), and its uneven brick floor is "the pulse of the house," says Rose Mary.

A native Australian, Rose Mary became totally addicted to green chile when she came to New Mexico. "I don't know what is is," she muses. "You smell it roasting at the market, and it's irresistible." She prefers milder chile, and she likes to put it in eggs and casseroles. She has only one rule of cooking. "My great rule is: taste all along," she says. "When cooking, you must use your own 'nous,' as we say in Australia. It's Greek for mind." Rose Mary developed her recipe for Sun-Dried Tomato Salsa because she "had more tomatoes than she knew what to do with."

Sun-Dried Tomato Salsa

2 cups canned tomatoes
2 fresh tomatoes, cut into chunks
1 medium red onion, cut into chunks
1 teaspoon coarse ground red chile
3 shakes wine vinegar
Squeeze of lemon ½ tsp. salt
1 well-packed cup of sun-dried tomatoes
3 tablespoons cilantro, finely chopped, optional

1-2 teaspoons extra virgin olive oil
2 cloves garlic
5-6 green chiles, roasted and peeled (if using canned, use hot chiles)
1 chile pequin, crushed with rolling pin
4 stems parsley
6 or so basil leaves
Finely chopped black and green olives, optional

Drizzle olive oil on sun-dried tomatoes. Put aside. Put canned and fresh tomatoes in blender. Blend. Add onion (save a little bit). Blend. Add a sprinkling of fresh parsley and a touch of fresh basil, red chile, wine vinegar, lemon juice and salt. Blend for 30 seconds. Pour ½ mixture into pot. Bring to rollicking boil, stirring occasionally. While cooking, add to remaining mixture in blender most of the sun-dried tomatoes (save a few). Blend, with garlic, for 2-3 minutes. As other half of mixture is boiling, add the mixture remaining in the blender to pot. Stir. Add chopped green chile and chile pequin. Let salsa continue to reduce. Add very finely chopped parsley, basil and remaining sun-dried tomatoes. Boil down for 15 minutes, or until thickened. Add optional olives and/or cilantro at very end.
Makes 2 cups.

Salsa Fresca con Chipotle

Dan Wells and Kathy Grassel

People like to drop in on Dan Wells and Kathy Grassel; there's no need to call ahead. It can be a tight squeeze between the kitchen table and the stove. That's because, on so many evenings, friends are seated around the scarred, round old oak table, talking movies, politics and relationships, planning the next cross-country ski trip or camping trip, depending on the season—and munching chips slathered with the fine salsa Dan conjures up. Urban pioneers, Kathy and Dan bought their 104-year-old house in Huning Highlands, a downtown Albuquerque neighborhood, almost a decade ago, and the kitchen has always been a haven for their wide circle of friends. Around the kitchen table have passed countless stories of romances, break-ups, marathon runs, job interviews and foreign travels. If anyone asks, Dan and Kathy's kitchen is where the '60s have landed.

Food tends to appear like magic in this kitchen. Dan is the chef at Conrad's, a downtown restaurant, but that doesn't stop him from fixing memorable feasts for his friends on his nights off. When he ran a cafe in Central City, Colorado, during the '70s, he was known as "Hamburger Dan," and he claims to have worked "everywhere" from truck stops to fancy restaurants.

Dan's been experimenting with salsa for years. One of his favorites, Salsa Fresca con Chipotle, warms the inside of your mouth to a hum. He likes this recipe especially well because "the smokiness of the mezcal matches the pecan wood-smoked chipotle."

Salsa Fresca con Chipotle

½ red onion, diced
3 cups fresh tomatoes, diced
2 tablespoons chopped cilantro
4 chipotle peppers, hydrated and minced
   (canned or dried)
1 teaspoon salt
1 teaspoon sugar
Juice of one lime
A few drops mezcal

Remove seeds and stems from the chipotles. Hydrate the dried chipotles by placing them in enough water to cover. Bring them to a boil, turn off the heat and let them sit until they cool. After mincing them finely, add all the ingredients together. Let the salsa sit for at least a half-hour before serving. This is the perfect salsa to serve with cold Mexican beer at a summer barbeque.

TOASTED CHILE PEQUIN SALSA

Tonie Apodaca

"This is the salsa I've been eating all my life," says the 70 year-old Tonie Apodaca, which is about how long she's been performing the traditional music of Northern New Mexico on her guitar and accordian at village fiestas and weddings. She still lives in the three-room adobe house where she was born, in Rociada. "I live happy in this house," she says. "I like to stay where I can cook my own way." Pictures and statues of saints, family photographs, china cows and chickens and her accumulated honors fill every available inch of shelf and wall space. One stands out, a plaque from the city of Las Vegas, New Mexico: *Tonie Apodaca—Living Legend.*

The tiny, sprightly woman with coal-black hair feeds another log into the wood stove, heating it to exactly the right temperature to make tortillas. She mixes the dough, rolls out a monster-sized tortilla and flops it directly on top of the stove. When bubbles form, she grabs it and turns it over. "There's nothing like fresh salsa and fresh tortillas!" she exclaims.

Born to a family of professional musicians, music is with her always. When she's not playing her guitar or composing (by ear), she's humming aloud and waltzing about her kitchen as she cooks.

She places the chile pequins in a pie tin and toasts them very carefully in the wood stove for a brief minute, just until fragrant. She then places them outside the front door to cool. Meanwhile, she gets ready to chop them. "My mother didn't believe in blenders," she says. "She thought they took away the flavor." So Tonie places them in a glass jar and pounds them with a bolillo, an all-purpose tool also used for rolling tortillas, that looks like eight inches of a broom handle. She grinds the pequins by hand with a twisting motion, until they are reduced to a coarse powder. Tonie serves this salsa for dinner, on top of a simple and satisfying meal of beans and a baked potato, adding a sliced fresh jalapeño.

If you like your salsa red hot, this is the one for you. And remember: Tonie says she's never been to a doctor in her life!

Toasted Chile Pequin Salsa

I ounce chile pequins, toasted until
   fragrant, then ground by hand

8 ounces tomato sauce
4 ounces water
I small onion, chopped

Mix all ingredients, adding a pinch of salt.

Roadside Red Salsa

Cordelia Martinez

In the spring, at Eastertime, thousands of the faithful may be seen walking alongside the New Mexico roads, making their annual pilgrimage to the Santuario de Chimayo: then, in the fall, thousands more pilgrims arrive—this time in search of another kind of religious experience—that celebration of the senses which may be found in the consumption of the best chile. Up and down the road leading to this legendary 1813 Spanish Pueblo church are roadside chile sellers. Just as many old-time New Mexicans believe in the healing properties of the "holy dirt" found in the Chimayo chapel, so do they believe that along this road is where you can find the very best chile.

On the narrow road that leads toward the chapel, you will find Cordelia Martinez. From the back of her pickup truck, she offers the gifts of the earth: red chile, in thick ristras hung like a jeweled curtain from a cottonwood tree; crisp apples and baskets of plump, gleaming green chile, too. Open a bag of Mrs. Martinez' fresh-ground red chile and become intoxicated with the perfume of this "red gold."

This industrious woman with steel-gray curls does a brisk business, bargaining with the out-of-staters and chatting with the serious chile eaters as well, like the aged woman leaning on a cane from nearby Picuris Pueblo, who comes to buy from her every year. Business here is fast and serious, but she always finds a moment to joke with her customers. "Bargains, bargains," she exclaims to the passerbys. "I ground this myself, yesterday," she says, answering every question tossed at her, like a high official conducting a press conference.

"When I make salsa," says Cordelia, "I like to mix different kinds of chiles. You have to taste as you go. I like it not too hot. When I make this salsa, I eat it all up by myself!"

Roadside Red

I 14½ ounce can tomatoes
I jalapeño
I fresh green chile
I clove garlic
½ onion, chopped
½ teaspoon oregano
I teaspoon Chimayo red chile,
   coarse ground

I tablespoon fresh parsley, chopped
I tablespoon fresh cilantro, chopped
Salt to taste

Chop the tomatoes fine, into bite-size pieces. Chop the jalapeño, green chile and onion very small. Mince the garlic and chop the parsley and cilantro very fine. Mix all ingredients together. Let the salsa sit for a few hours before serving.

CORIANDER RELISH

Sallie Janpol

Known as one of Albuquerque's outstanding cooks, Sallie Janpol is perhaps most famous for her hand-dipped chocolate truffles and her extravagant birthday cakes, labors of love which can take as long as a week to create.

The chic yet comfortable kitchen where Sallie practices her food artistry is a clean, dramatic space. Opalescent black and white tiles line the white oak-floored room. Illuminated cabinets along the walls display her diverse china collection, which ranges all the way from Betty Boop to hand-painted Italian and Portugese platters in bright blues and yellows to her traditional gilt-edged wedding china. With its all-purpose, black and white marbled granite island, as fit for informal dining as for rolling pastry dough, this kitchen is "designed to keep the cook company."

A native New Mexican who insists that dishes cooked with chile be supremely flavorful as well as picante, Sallie, in her years of concocting elegant dinner parties, has become a spice artist. She never serves food that is ordinary; and, in her hands, even the familiar takes on a fresh twist. For birthdays, anniversaries, superbowls or at screenings of the latest video, Sallie loves to gather her friends together.

A dish that frequently appears on Sallie's table for family dinners as well as buffet parties is her Coriander Relish. The careful preparation of this condiment, with its hints of East India, rewards the taster with a burst of lively flavor that brightens up and compliments, but does not overwhelm grilled fish, baked or broiled chicken, roast lamb and pork. It can dress up a roast beef or turkey sandwich and may be combined with cream cheese for an omelette filling.

Like so many of Sallie's dishes, Coriander Relish makes use of perfectly ordinary ingredients with a taste surprise that is unique. Sallie likes to serve this brilliant red-orange relish in a simple white china bowl, at room temperature. It benefits from slow simmering.

Coriander Relish

3 lbs. roma tomatoes
¾ cup sweet red onion
¼ cup olive oil
2 bunches fresh coriander (cilantro)
1 chopped, seeded jalapeño
1 teaspoon salt
½ teaspoon cumin powder, lightly toasted
Juice of 1 large lime

Prepare the cumin by placing it on foil in a 200° degree oven for 5 minutes, or until fragrant, watching it very closely. Remove the skins of the tomatoes by plunging them into boiling water for 2-3 minutes. After removing the skins, core and chop them. Add diced onion to olive oil and cook over very low heat. Place the coriander in food processor or blender with one cup water for 1-2 minutes, just until finely chopped. Place the coriander in a sieve or colander, and press it to extract juice. Add this "coriander juice" to the tomato-onion mixture, then add the jalapeño, cumin and salt. Take care that no coriander gets into the mixture, as it will turn black and bitter. Cook over medium heat, at least 45 minutes, stirring occasionally, until it cooks down and thickens. Add the lime juice at the end of the cooking. Makes approximately 2 cups and keeps well for one week.

WILDFIRE SALSA

Michael Martin Murphey

A resident of Taos since 1978, singer-songwriter Michael Martin Murphey is a balladeer of "buckaroo old time cowboy tradition." With his recent album *Cowboy Songs: Rhymes of the Renegades*, a collection of 21 traditional cowpuncher tunes, he is aiming to "put western back with the word country." Adding to that ambition is his annual WestFest, held each summer in Red River, New Mexico, which is the closest event yet to Buffalo Bill Cody's Wild West Show, with its displays of horsemanship, trick-riding, music, cowboy poetry and traditional food.

When Michael gets together with the crowd of cowboys, Indians, artists, mountain men, craftspeople, and musicians who gather at his home or Wildfire Studio in Taos, he's likely to bring out his Wildfire Salsa for the occasion. It's easy to fix, just hot enough, and there won't be any leftovers. This salsa is the perfect one to serve to company that just drops in, as it can be put together in just a half-hour from what you have in the cupboard.

Murphey's Wildfire Salsa

2 onions, chopped
3 cloves garlic, minced
2 tablespoons vegetable oil
2-14½ once cans crushed tomatoes
1-7 once can chopped hot green chile
1 tablespoon cumin
1 teaspoon salt

Cook onions and garlic in oil until soft. Add tomatoes and chile. Simmer until thick. Add cumin and salt to taste. Cool and serve.

GARLIC-MARINATED GREEN CHILE RELISH

Eloise Henry

Raton, New Mexico, hasn't changed all that much since 1945, when Eloise Henry arrived. Perched on the northern edge of New Mexico, overlooking Raton Pass into Colorado, it's still the quintessential western small town, inhabited by ranchers, miners, railroaders and their families. Many children of the original settler families still live here. Mornings, old-timers gather at Johnny's Bakery on Second Street—where, when you ask for a cinnamon roll, the waitress asks if you want it baked or fried.

Eloise's kitchen hasn't changed much, either. Her collection of fancy plates from different states has grown, filling the display shelves all the way around the room, where rosy-ckeeked Victorian maidens smile from period Coca-Cola memorabilia. It's *de riguer* to take your time with several cups of coffee around the kitchen table in the morning; proper attire for guests is a fuzzy robe. In fact, Raton, New Mexico, may well be the fuzzy robe capital of the world.

Garlic-Marinated Green Chile Relish is one of Eloise's "favorite ways of eating chile." She's been fixing her chiles this way for 30 years, and she says "you know it's ready when you can smell the garlic." She thinks it's "good with anything, especially a peanut butter sandwich."

When the Italians arrived in the early part of this century to work in the coal mines, they brought with them their traditional recipes. Garlic-Marinated Green Chile Relish is a superb marriage between these Italian influences and native Hispanic tastes and ingredients.

Garlic-Marinated Green Chile Relish

12-15 firm, meaty green New Mexico
  chiles, roasted and peeled
2-3 garlic cloves, minced
Olive oil to cover
¼ cup balsamic or red wine vinegar

Combine all ingredients and stir well.
Let stand one week in the refrigerator
in a covered jar. Goes well as a condiment
on hamburgers, roast meat, eggs.
Keeps very well.

Mayan Kings' Chocolate-Chile Dip with Five-Spice Tortillas

W.C. Longacre - Mountain Road Cafe

The originator of "New Hong Key" cuisine, W.C. Longacre brings to his kitchen his three great loves—New Mexican, Oriental and Caribbean cuisine. He serves an inventive menu that delightfully mixes his 20-plus years of restauranting in Albuquerque and Key West, traveling throughout Central America and Mexico, and studying in Hong Kong. At W.C.'s Mountain Road Cafe, he practices his Pacific Rim-oriented progressive fusion cuisine. Located on the very edge of Albuquerque's Old Town, this off-the-beaten-path cafe is exactly the sort of hidden treasure those who love seeking new dining experiences dream of finding.

"I restaurant for the privilege of cooking what I want to cook," he says. With his silvering pony tail and beard, his twinkling blue eyes, and his irrepressible energy, you'd be willing to follow the puckish W.C. just about anywhere, because there's no doubt that wherever he's going, that's where the party is.

His Mayan Kings' Chocolate-Chile Dip is the result of a series of desserts he played with. "Chocolate and chile are a wonderful marriage," this lover of red chile fudge believes. (He had read of a Mayan court drink described as a red chile chocolate milk, of which 50 casks a day were consumed.) In addition to serving as a dip for the Five Spice Tortillas or an assortment of fresh strawberries, pineapple, bananas, pound cake and ladyfingers, he recommends serving it over crepes stuffed with poached pears.

"This luscious, elegant dessert is simplicity itself to prepare," he says, allowing you to spend more time with your guests. W.C. likes to serve it accompanied with a spicy wine, like a Gewürztraminer.

Mayan Kings' Chocolate-Chile Dip With Five-Spice Tortillas

8 ounces milk chocolate (Ghiradelli is good: just avoid paraffin-based products)
1 teaspoon powdered sugar
¼ teaspoon cinnamon
1-2 tablespoons finely-ground Chimayo red chile
½ teaspoon vanilla extract
(Mexican vanilla if available)
½ cup whipping cream

Break chocolate into 1-inch pieces. Add chocolate and all remaining ingredients, except whipping cream in a fondue pot, chaffing dish or double boiler. While blending over low heat, slowly add whipping cream as chocolate melts, until mixture is completely smooth. If it becomes too thick, it can be thinned with the addition of a bit of warm cream or milk. Serves 6.

Five-Spice Tortillas

½ dozen or so whole wheat tortillas
2 eggs
2 ounces milk
¼ teaspoon vanilla extract
   (Mexican if available)
1 teaspoon five-spice powder (from
   local Chinese market, if possible)

Blend last four ingredients with a whisk.
Dip the tortillas, one by one, in the batter,
or brush with a pastry brush. Cook on
medium-hot griddle or cast iron skillet in
light vegetable oil. Refresh oil as necessary.
Cook one minute on first side, then turn;
cook ½ minute on other side. Blot on paper
towel. Stack tortillas and cut into quarters.

PAPAYA HABANERO SALSA

*W.C. Longacre-*Mountain Road Cafe

For that fire-eating friend who can be counted on to say, "It's not hot enough," try serving Papaya Habanero Salsa. Its creator, Albuquerque chef W.C. Longacre, promises that it will take the curl out of a perm. This tropical blend is "for the brave," he says, but, "once you're into habaneros, there's no going back." This, remember, comes from a man who likes his chile first thing in the morning.

Memories of time spent in Barbados inspired W.C. to create this salsa, namely some "very crispy fresh fish served with an intensely hot preparation."

Sweet, fragrant, with a glowing golden color, this salsa looks deceptively innocent. Don't be fooled. It's not meant to be served with chips. Instead, this salsa does well when drizzled over a simply breaded and fried chicken breast or fish fillet. W.C. also recommends this salsa as a "perfect palate stimulator," and sees serving it as a light first course on grilled chicken kabobs skewered with melon balls and orange wedges. The papaya enzyme helps the digestion and will keep you out of trouble, despite the heat.

Papaya Habanero Salsa

¾ pound ripe papaya pulp,
    skin and seeds removed
1½ tablespoons fresh habaneros,
    seeds and stems removed
1 large garlic clove
1½ tablespoons seedless raisins
½ medium yellow onion, quartered
⅛ teaspoon vanilla
    (preferably Mexican)
⅛ teaspoon fresh ground Jamaican
    allspice, coarsely ground with
    mortar and pestle
2 tablespoons white wine vinegar
1 tablespoon white sugar
½ teaspoon salt
Pinch cinnamon
1 tablespoon cornstarch

2 cups water
¾ tablespoon brown sugar

Add all ingredients except last 5 in food processor. Process so mixture is well-blended but retains texture. Place mixture in saucepan with 1½ cup water on medium-high heat. Mix remaining ½ cup water with cornstarch. Set aside. Add cinnamon and brown sugar to papaya mixture as it begins to boil, stirring frequently. When it comes to a high simmer, add the corn-starch mixture, stirring first. Then, stirring frequently, cook on low boil for 7 minutes, or until it thickens. Be careful to keep it from sticking. Set aside overnight. This freezes indefinitely and keeps in the refrigerator up to 6 weeks.

BASIL-SMOKED PASILLA CREAM DIP

Elizabeth Berry

Pink celery, white carrots, black tomatoes and orange watermelon all bloom into existence with the help of Abiquiu grower Elizabeth Berry's extraordinary green thumb. She grows exotic vegetables for 14 of Santa Fe's poshest restaurants, and she does it by hand, from planting to delivery. "I don't have a tractor," she says. "We hoe by hand; it's all done by hand."

This 58-year old mother of five, her silver hair tied back with orange yarn, rarely sits still; her passion for her newly-discovered role as "seed guardian" animating her face and her exhuberent flow of words. "I grow for seed banks. . . . Those are the real saints—the gardeners out there who are saving the seeds!"

To walk through her living room is to tiptoe around baskets of dried chiles, beans of wonderfully assorted speckles and shapes and piles of seeds drying on blankets stretched out on the floor. "I don't grow ordinary chiles," she says, holding up a ristra of glowing purple, gold and orange-hued peppers. Some of her chiles, like the long slender pasilla negra, she smokes over basil wood, the dried stems of basil that are left after the leaves are picked.

After raising her family in Berkeley, California, Elizabeth and husband Fred found their Gallina Canyon Ranch, 20 miles out on a dirt road, in the heart of red-cliffed Georgia O'Keeffe country above Abiquiu. "There's no phone, no electricity and no gas," Elizabeth says. "Our nearest neighbors are the monks at Christ in the Desert Monastery." It took the Berrys ten years to build their ranch house with its 22-inch thick adobe walls.

In her kitchen, with its pine cabinets, Mexican tile counters and latilla ceilings, Elizabeth cooks by candlelight on a wood stove.

When she serves Basil-Smoked Pasilla Cream, she says people "just go wild. They can't figure out what it is! Believe me, this is a killer dip."

Basil-Smoked Pasilla Cream Dip

4-6 basil-smoked pasillas
1 cup yogurt
1 cup sour cream
6-8 slices bacon

Toast the pasillas very carefully, about 30 seconds per side, just until they begin to become fragrant. A toaster-oven works well for this, because you can move very quickly. Break off their stems, crunch them, and put them in simmering water to reconstitute, about 10 minutes. After they cook, run the pasillas through the blender. You can add a little cornstarch to thicken the mixture. As the pasillas are simmering, fry the bacon very crisp. Blend pasilla paste and crumbled bacon with sour cream and yogurt. Great on potatoes, baked or home-fried, fish and pasta. (For a more low-fat version, use all yogurt and turkey bacon. If basil-smoked pasillas are not available, ordinary pasillas may be used.)

CHILE PHILLY DIP

Peggy Otero Schmidt

As the descendent of one of New Mexico's most prominent old families, Peggy Otero Schmidt spent time as a child on her father's sheep ranch, learning one of New Mexico's traditional ways of life.

While growing up, Peggy spent summers in Tesuque, above Santa Fe, where she now lives with her daughter, Karen. Together, they are restoring their adobe home, designed by William Penhallow Henderson, the architect responsible for much of Santa Fe's character. It was the home of Albert Schmidt, Karen's grandfather, a member of the Santa Fe art colony of the 1920s and 1930s.

When Karen, a Chicago television executive, inherited the home from her grandmother five years ago, she made an astonishing discovery. Hidden in the garage of the classic 1920s adobe were hundreds of Albert Schmidt's paintings, locked away at the time of his death in 1957. Now that the paintings have been restored and brought back to life, Schmidt is gaining recognition as the "lost pintor," or the missing "sixth" member of Santa Fe's acclaimed Los Cinco Pintores, the modernists who captured the special light and landscapes of northern New Mexico during the early part of the century.

Peggy and Karen haven't yet had the opportunity to restore the tiny kitchen, but they manage quite well at giving splendid, informal dinner parties for small groups of friends. On those candlelit nights, laughter peals forth, wine flows, the flames flicker, and who knows? Perhaps the ghosts of Santa Fe's esteemed artists and writers are called back to this spacious dining room, where they once enjoyed such dinner parties, lending a glimmer of their high spirits.

Peggy suggests this piquant recipe as a "chile initiation" for those who may be just starting out on their chile careers, or for those who prefer their chile mild rather than wild.

Chile Philly Dip

8 ounces cream cheese, softened
2 fresh green New Mexico chiles, roasted, peeled and chopped, without seeds
8 green, pimento-stuffed olives, chopped
3 scallions, finely chopped

Cream all ingredients into the cream cheese. Add a little milk if the mixture is too thick. Mound into a peak and sprinkle with paprika. In addition to serving this dip with crackers, Peggy likes to use it as a sandwich filling, or as a stuffing for celery stalks.

The photo opposite shows a kitchen typical of homes in the Tesuque region.

PRIZE GUACAMOLE DIP

Josie Gallegos - Josie's

For the past 25 years, not only have people waited in line to eat at Josie's, they have been happy to do so. A visit to this modest lunchroom on East Marcy Street was as essential to the Santa Fe experience as a stroll around the Plaza. When Josie went into retirement in the late summer of 1993, there was general mourning in the city. This event was deemed a sign that the fall of Santa Fe was imminent. What would we do without Josie's fantastic chile (both red and green), indescribable desserts (mocha cake, Russian cream pie), wonderful waitresses who knew your name, and prices so reasonable they seemed miraculous? Josie's cooking was not only "just like Mom's," it was much, much better!

All is not lost, however. Josie has since emerged from her brief retirement, and she is once again open in her Marcy St. house—for what many people believe, even after all these years, and the hundreds of restaurants that have come and gone, is the best Mexican food in Santa Fe.

Prize Guacamole Dip

3 ripe avocado pears
Juice of 1 lemon
1 tablespoon onion juice
1 clove garlic, mashed
4-6 tablespoon finely chopped
   celery or green pepper

1 tbs. finely chopped fresh
   parsley or cilantro
Salt and freshly ground black pepper
½ teaspoon Chimayo red chile,
   finely ground, to taste

Mash the avocados with a fork. Add the other ingredients and mix well. Serve immediately with tortilla chips.

TESUQUE GARDEN GUACAMOLE DIP

Linda Pontecorvo

Tesuque, the picturesque community just north of Santa Fe, has in recent years become known as a haven for superstars. Long inhabited by artists and old-timers, bordering the site of an Indian pueblo, the town is now attempting to weather the changes brought by its increasing popularity without losing its character. One constant that unites newcomers and old-timers alike is the love of their gardens. Bright blossoms, often planted to appear "wild," reward the careful tending demanded by the high altitude and short growing season.

Linda Pontecorvo tends some of Tesuque's glorious gardens. She has, in the past, gardened extensively in New Zealand and run a bouganvilla nursery in Australia. "I'm not a cook—I'm a gardener" she insists, because her cooking depends entirely on what's available fresh from the garden. Her great love is fresh herbs, and when they are in season, she believes in eating them plentifully, "like a green." Fresh herbs are the key to her Tesuque Garden Guacamole. This creamy, piquant dip is heaven and its rich creaminess stands out particularly well when served in combination with one or two spicier salsas. Decorate the top with sprigs of fresh herbs and carrot curls—and raves are guaranteed. Just try not to "sample" too much before serving—or this one might not make it out of the kitchen.

Tesuque Garden Guacamole Dip

I ripe avocado
2 oz. cream cheese, softened
¼ cup fresh tarragon or
   ¼ cup fresh dill, chopped
¼ cup fresh oregano, chopped

Juice of ½ fresh lime
½ tsp. balsamic vinegar
½ tsp. olive oil
½ tsp. Chimayo red chile,
   finely ground, to taste

Mash the avocado with the cream cheese. Add the other ingredients. Mix well. Serve immediately with blue corn chips.

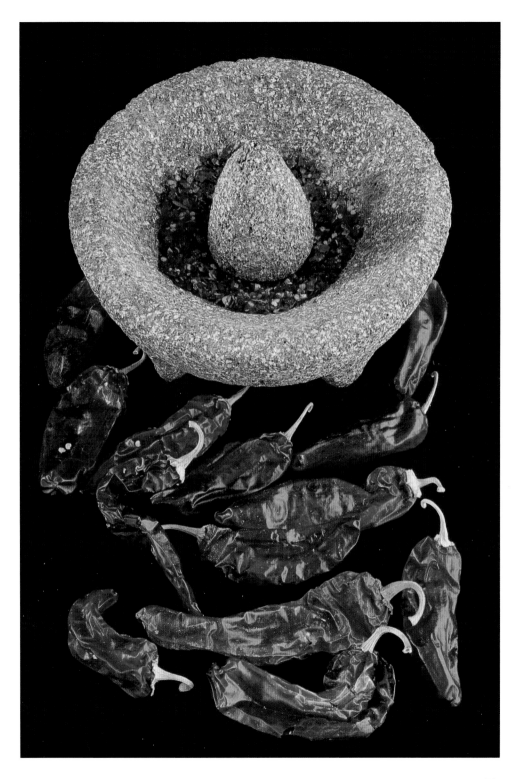

HOT-STUFF DIP

Carmella Padilla

A mong her friends, writer Carmella Padilla admits she holds a "reputation" for favoring chile that hits the upper end of the blister scale. However, when she goes to parties, Carmella brings huge quantities of this truly addictive sour cream-based dip, which inevitably disappear. She doesn't know the origins of the recipe; she says it is "something that her family always made." The taste is far more than the sum of its simple parts.

As vice-president of the Spanish Colonial Arts Society, the organization founded in 1925 for the preservation and promotion of traditional New Mexico village crafts—tinwork, weaving, straw applique, colcha embroidery and woodcarving—Carmella, a lifelong Santa Fean, works actively to preserve the culture of this region. Each year at Christmastime, she loves to join her mother and aunts in the preparation of vast quantities of posole, tamales, pastelitos and other holiday delicacies. There, in her mother's fragrant kitchen, Carmella laughs, jokes, and gossips with the older women of her family, who share with her stories of long ago. Together, they prepare soul-warming treats, the taste of which, blessedly, never changes. Taking a break from this delightful "women's ritual," they enjoy a snack of Carmella's fresh-tasting green chili dip.

Carmella's Hot-Stuff Dip

I pint sour cream
I cup (8-12) fresh roasted and
   peeled New Mexico chile
   (or more, to taste)
½ teaspoon garlic salt

After roasting and peeling the chiles, refrigerate them for an hour, then drain the juice. Mix the chiles with sour cream and garlic salt. Refrigerate at least ½ hour to allow the flavors to blend. Serve with tortilla and potato chips. It works well as a dip for fresh vegetables or as an omelette filling. Carmella believes this dip improves with age. It will keep one week in the refrigerator.

JALAPEÑO DIP

Max Evans

Cowboy, rancher, miner, artist, novelist and screenwriter Max Evans is perhaps best-known as author of *The Rounders*, starring Henry Fonda and Glenn Ford. Evans is the author of 16 books. His personal history reads like a western saga: a working cowboy by the time he was 12, he ran his cow ranch in Union County while still in his teens. After serving in World War II, he settled in Taos and painted, then switched to writing. He's been to Hollywood—where he wrote many Western film scripts—and back, and he now lives in Albuquerque.

"I had to cook sometimes when I was a 'lil ol' cowboy," he says, "and jalapeños—I could eat 'em every day."

"This is my favorite," he says of his Jalapeño Dip. "I have a great feeling for jalapeños. And this recipe is absolutely original," he guarantees, just like his latest novel, *Bluefeather Fellini*, about a half-Italian, half-Taos Pueblo Indian miner's lifelong quest for gold.

Max likes to make a batch of this dip and stuff jalapeños with it to serve as an appetizer. "We have it when someone we love comes by, or people from out of town," he says. What he does is cut jalapeños in half, remove the seeds and pith, and fill the halves with the dip mixture. "Sprinkle with paprika for added color," he says. He and his wife Pat have been serving these stuffed jalapeños for years in their Albuquerque home, but, he says, "damned if I know where this came from! But I love it, and I have spread the word."

"No doubt about it," says Max, try this Jalapeño Dip and "you truly will get addicted to it."

Jalapeño Dip

1-8 ounce package cream cheese,
    at room temperature
¼ teaspoon Lowry's Original
    Seasoned Salt
½-1 teaspoon minced fresh cilantro
1 canned or pickled jalapeño,
    seeded and minced
Just enough milk to achieve the
    right consistency

Mix all the ingredients. If serving as a spread rather than a dip, add a small amount of milk to thin slightly.

BLACK BEAN DIP

Dan Wells - Conrad's Restaurant

Hotelier Conrad Hilton grew up in the small town of San Antonio, New Mexico, where his family ran a boarding house, and dreamed of opening a world-class hotel in his home state. He fulfilled that dream when he opened La Posada—the very first Hilton hotel—in downtown Albuquerque in 1939. At the time, its ten stories made it the tallest building in New Mexico—and it boasted the first elevator. And when he married Zsa Zsa Gabor, he brought his new bride to La Posada, overlooking the crossroads of Route 66 and a key stop on the Atchison, Topeka & Santa Fe Railroad line.

Today, Dan Wells is chef in Conrad's, the restaurant located in La Posada, named for the hotel's founder. Dan serves a sophisticated combination of Spanish and Yucatan dishes in the restored cafe, blending nostalgia with an assortment of awakened tastes travelers appreciate. One of the most requested items on the menu is his Black Bean Soup; Dan plays with the recipe by turning soup into Black Bean Dip. Using the same seasonings and modifying the texture, Dan creates a basic dip that pleases a wide range of palates and goes well as an appetizer with just about any main dish. Black beans are delicious on their own, and when prepared by slow cooking in garlic and ginger, then pureed with spicy jalapeños, they result in a dip that anyone can eat and everyone will.

Black Bean Dip

The Soup

1 pound black beans
6 quarts water
3 cloves garlic, smashed
1 thumb-sized piece of ginger root
1 large onion, diced
3 carrots, diced
½ bunch celery, diced
¼ pound ham, diced (optional)
1 tablespoon whole thyme
1 teaspoon cayenne
2 teaspoons Tobasco sauce
¼ cup Port
Zest of 2 lemons
Salt

Wash and sort the beans, then soak them overnight. Add the water, garlic, ginger and onion and bring to a boil, then simmer 2 hours. Then add the carrots, celery, ham, thyme and cayenne. Simmer one more hour, then add the Tobasco and Port. When beans are tender and done, add lemon zest and salt to taste.

Black Bean Dip

2 cups cooked black beans (from soup)
2 scallions, chopped
3-5 jalapeños, chopped,
     seeds and stems removed
½ cup grated white cheese
     (Monterey Jack or Queso Blanco)

Take two cups cooked black beans from soup. Puree, but before you do, remove lemon zest and ginger first. Add scallions, jalapeños and cheese, mixing by hand. Salt and pepper to taste. Serve with corn chips and an assortment of sliced red and green peppers, carrots, broccoli, jicama, radishes, celery, zucchini, cherry tomatoes and other fresh vegetables.

HOMEMADE RED CHILE MAYONNAISE

Sallie Janpol

Every cook needs a few tricks hidden up the sleeve; a dish or two that can transform an otherwise ordinary meal into a special event. Then, while graciously accepting the raves, you, the magician, can think to yourself, "If they only knew how easy this was."

You ought to consider adding Homemade Red Chile Mayonnaise to your repertoire of trickery. It's a technique that is easily mastered. Your own mayo will have a clarity and a silky texture that can make even humble tuna fish remarkable. And when you add red chile, the piquancy of the spice plays out brilliantly with the creamy subtlety of the mayonnaise.

Sallie Janpol says her red chile mayonnaise is fabulous with chicken salad, egg salad, hamburgers, cold cuts and fresh vegetables, making it ideal to serve at a buffet. As someone who loves to entertain, and does so often, Sallie relies on her "magic" file. She's served her red chile mayonnaise at some of her most memorable parties.

Homemade Red Chile Mayonnaise

The Red Chile

2 tablespoons vegetable oil
3 garlic cloves, minced
2-3 tablespoons Chimayo red chile (finely ground)
2 cups warm chicken stock (homemade, or a good commercial brand)
½ teaspoon cumin

Barely heat the vegetable oil. Add the garlic cloves and saute gently 3-5 minutes. Add the chile powder. Stir 2-3 minutes on low-medium heat. Gradually add the warm chicken stock, stirring constantly. Add cumin. Cook 10 minutes on low, stirring occasionally. Let this cool.

The Mayonnaise

2 egg yolks
1½ teaspoon Dijon mustard
1 tablespoon wine vinegar or lemon juice
⅓ cup olive oil
Salt and pepper to taste

Place all ingredients except last two in blender or food processor. As they are blending, start adding the olive oil, drop by drop, until it is all incorporated and the mayonnaise has thickened. This takes about 3 minutes. The secret is having patience and slowly drizzling the oil. This makes about two cups.

When the red chile has cooled completely, add ¼ cup of it to the mayonnaise, mix and taste for seasonings.

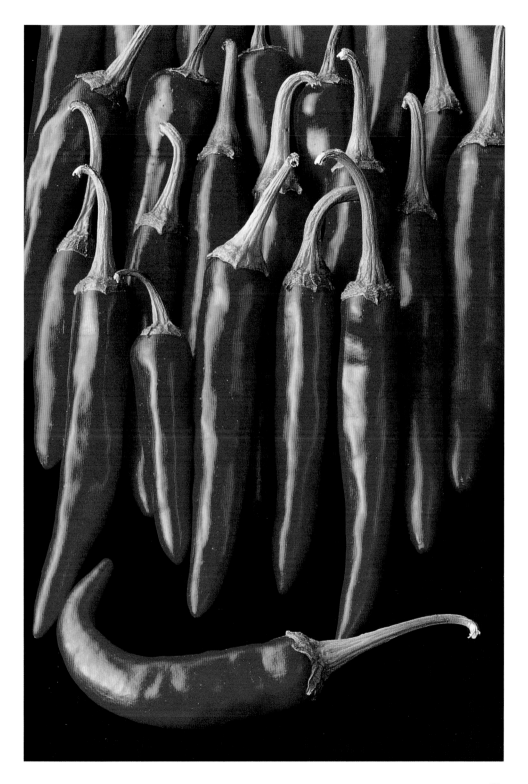

CARNE ADOVADA MARINADE

Bea Montoya-M & J's Sanitary Tortilla Factory

Maybe not all of Albuquerque eats lunch at M & J's. But so much of the city shows up here regularly, you're sure to run into several old friends any day of the week. Positioned on the very edge of downtown, M & J's attracts a faithful crowd of lawyers, university types, old-timers, downtown folks, artists and reporters, as well as increasing numbers of national and international visitors. "We get at least 200-300 customers a week from other countries," says owner Bea Montoya.

The postcards, notes and snapshots stapled to the walls tell the story: "The best Mexican food . . ." they proclaim, from Switzerland, Japan, Africa. Many semi-natives, including the author of this cookbook, learned to eat chile at M & J's. And the wonderful part is, M & J's never changes. It was great 10 years ago, and it's just as great today. Consistency is Bea's credo, a divine doctrine that includes health-conscious preparation that foregoes the use of oil or lard, and the demonstration of big-hearted hospitality that guarantees a hug and warm "How are you today?" every time you show up.

Bea and her husband, Jake, have created a genuine "home away from home" for the whole city. Starting out 18 years ago in a small hole-in-the-wall, M & J's today is a light, bright, open bustling lunchroom that seats 180. From the walls, works by local artists, the saints and the Virgin of Guadalupe grant their blessings upon the diners blissfully munching New Mexico's soul food.

"Green chile almost anyone can make," says Bea. "But red chile—red chile is harder. Always add your spices at the beginning of your simmer."

M & J's Carne Adovada is long-simmered to tenderness, bathed in a glorious, savory sauce, deeply spiced with comino.

Carne Adovada Marinade

Red Chile Sauce

¾ pound Hatch red chile pods
1 tablespoon salt
Water

Soak the pods in lukewarm water with the salt for 1 and ½ hours. Shake out the seeds and drain. Place pods in blender with some of the soaking water and puree. Bring the chile puree to a boil, add 2 and ½ cups water, keeping the texture not too thick and not too watery. Simmer 35-40 minutes on very low heat, watching carefully, like a pudding, and stirring frequently.

Marinade

2 pints red chile sauce (above)

3 tablespoons granulated garlic

¼ teaspoon oregano

**1 and ½ teaspoons whole comino
(cumin) seeds**

**2 pounds boneless cushion pork, cut into
bite-size pieces and boiled for 3 hours;
or substitute beef such as sirloin or top
round, boiling one hour.**

Mix the garlic, oregano, comino and chile
sauce. Marinate meat in this mixture for two
hours. Simmer on very low heat for 45
minutes, until very tender, stirring frequently.
Serve wrapped in corn, blue corn or flour
tortillas, topped with red or green chile. If
you can't decide, have both!

SWEET-HOT SESAME MARINADE

Sharon Niederman

This Oriental-fragranced marinade does wonderful things not only for chicken and beef, but vegetables as well. Try pouring it over boiled new potatoes or a mixture of snow peas and jicama, then let the vegetables sit in the refrigerator overnight. It also doubles as a salad dressing. And it makes the very best chicken salad when used as an overnight marinade on sliced poached chicken breasts.

While the origins of this recipe are shrouded in mystery, legend has it that when the face of the Madonna appeared on the tortilla, the first thing she requested was chile. The villagers of the tiny town of Loco Caliente, New Mexico, attempted to concoct a dish that would satisfy her. Fortunately, the humble native pequin growing outside in the garden was available, that same chile pequin that heats up the salsas of the New World and the stir frys of the Orient.

While traversing the backroads of the Land of Enchantment, the author of this book had the opportunity to sample a chicken salad prepared with the villagers' glorious pequin-spiced marinade, with its savory mingling of sweet and heat. Somehow, she persuaded them to part with the marvelous recipe that highlights its sesame flavor with chile. Now, in her own sky blue-walled kitchen, hung with bright, tin-framed colcha embroideries, and collections of exotic chile peppers displayed in jars on the counters, she prepares spring and summer salads of crisp garden snow peas, brilliant green asparagus and new potatoes with Sweet-Hot Sesame Marinade. From her kitchen windows, she and her dinner guests watch as the Sandia Mountains turn watermelon-red for a precious few moments at sunset.

Sweet-Hot Sesame Marinade

¼ cup peanut oil
¼ cup cider vinegar
1 tablespoon sesame oil
1 tablespoon soy sauce
1-2 teaspoons sugar
3 crushed chile pequin
A big pinch salt

Combine all ingredients in a jar and shake very well. Let sit for an hour in the refrigerator for the flavors to blend. Marinate meats two hours; vegetables overnight.

GREEN CHILE DYNAMITE MARINADE

Chuck Henry

A dedicated outdoorsman, Chuck Henry originally developed this spicy marinade for game. Like many natives of northern New Mexico raised along its streams and rivers, growing up on its forested mountains, he learned early the importance of providing fish and meat from those rivers and mountains. A superb fly fisherman, in the summer he enjoys grilling trout from the San Juan or the Cimarron. During the colder months, he devises fresh ways to prepare venison, antelope, pheasant and quail he and his 16-year-old son, Eric, bring home. A major challenge is finding ways to fix this provender so it will be appealing to friends unaccustomed to the taste of wild game.

Looking for a way to remove the "gaminess" of venison, he masterminded a green chile marinade that ignites the flavors of grilled meats. This New Mexico native admits he is happily addicted to chile. "You know how it is," he says, "when it's chile season, you just want to use it everywhere!" While he customarily uses this recipe to prepare venison and antelope steaks and kabobs for the grill, some kitchen testing proves it works quite well on chicken and lamb, too. The chile heat, as well as the flavoring, completely permeates the chicken, leaving it with a warm, "roasty" glow.

And, Chuck points out, this marinade gives the cook a special opportunity—to nibble the charcoaled bits of chile while waiting for the meat to finish.

Green Chile Dynamite Marinade

1 cup olive oil
2 cups red wine
1 package onion soup mix
4 tablespoons Worcestshire sauce
1 well-packed cup (about 12) fresh
    roasted and peeled green
    New Mexico chiles
4 cloves garlic
⅛ teaspoon black pepper
Pinch oregano
Pinch cumin

Combine the olive oil, wine and onion soup and mix well. Add the Worcestshire sauce and coarsely chopped chiles. (Fresh is best, of course, but frozen will do.) Run the garlic through a garlic press, or mince very fine. Add the garlic and remaining ingredients. Mix well. Pierce meat and marinate two hours at room temperature, turning frequently. This marinade makes enough for two pounds of meat. Use the marinade to baste the meat while grilling.

RED CHILE-GINGER CHICKEN MARINADE

Kathy Grassel

When she settled down in New Mexico after years of working and living in Europe, Kathy Grassel wanted a garden. Raised on a farm in South Dakota, she knew how to make things grow. One big reason why she and her husband, chef Dan Wells, decided to buy their late-Victorian house was for the garden space it offered. While it started out as only a small backyard strip, over the years Dan and Kathy have created, in the midst of the city, an organic garden that supplies a respectable amount of their vegetables. They especially like to experiment with growing varieties of chiles, and their pequins, jalapeños and Big Jims flourish abundantly.

An expert at preparing big, spicy meals to satisfy the appetites of their many chile-loving friends, Kathy designed this pungent Red Chile-Ginger Marinade as a simple way to prepare chicken for the grill or the broiler. This marinade infuses the chicken with the irresistible mingled heats of the chile and the fresh ginger ("Use lots," says Kathy). If you prepare this dish in a wok or decide to saute the chicken, keep adding the marinade during your preparation. It will cook down and thicken, leaving a gold-orange sauce that looks spectacular when spooned over the chicken and arrayed on a plate with rice pilaf and fresh steamed broccoli.

Red Chile-Ginger Chicken Marinade

1 teaspoon (or more) fresh-grated
　　ginger root
¼ cup tamari
½ cup orange juice
2-3 tablespoons orange marmalade
　　(or any other sweet fruit preserve,
　　peach, pineapple or combination)
¼ cup cider vinegar
2 teaspoons finely ground Chimayo
　　red chile

Combine all ingredients, being careful to whisk in the marmalade until it is well-mixed. Pour over chicken and marinate in the refrigerator at least 4 hours, turning occasionally.

Triple Peppers con Queso

Chuck Henry

With this variation of the standard chile con queso, you get an extra crunch and a zesty new flavor. Look out though, if you're planning to serve it as an appetizer. Once you start, it is nearly impossible to stop eating. Triple Peppers con Queso was improvised over a campfire, one frigid November night. Arriving late at their campsite above Abiquiu on the Chama River, three hunters, after pitching their tents in the dark, were too tired to cook and too hungry to go to sleep. "It was deer season," recalls Chuck Henry, "and nobody felt like fixing supper. We tripped over enough pinon and cedar to build a fire, then we made a pot of coffee." Pulling out their supplies, they created this together in an old cast-iron skillet and cooked it over hot coals. "That queso tasted exceptionally good. We completely cleaned out that skillet!" he grins.

This queso still feels like a "guy-fixing" kind of dish, Chuck says, because you can just throw everything together and it still tastes great.

This recipe makes enough for eight people as an hors d'oeuvre or three guys during half-time. Kids love it, too, and warming it up in the microwave doesn't hurt it a bit.

Triple Peppers con Queso

3-4 chopped fresh green chiles,
    including seeds
1 jalapeño, finely-chopped, seeds removed
1 bell pepper chopped
1 small onion, chopped
4 cloves garlic, minced
½-lb. cheese, cubed

Lightly saute the vegetables in just enough oil to coat the bottom of the pan. Just as the vegetables are becoming soft (5-7 minutes), add the cheese, a little at a time. Heat briefly on low, just until the cheese melts. Keep this warm in a crockpot or fondue dish—or have the gang come and get it right off the stove. Serve with an assortment of fresh vegetables and chips. You can vary this dish by preparing it with cheddar or jack cheese. If it needs a bit of thinning, add a little evaporated milk.

HOT CHILE OIL

Seeds of Change

Sounding the call for "backyard biodiversity," Seeds of Change, a small Santa Fe seed company, now offers over 500 varieties of extremely interesting, certified organic plant possibilities for home gardeners. A look at their chile seed list provides a glimpse of the historical, international diversity Seeds of Change brings to the kitchen table: Bolivian Rainbow, Czechoslovakian Black, Española Improved, Peruvian Purple, Aji Habanero—these are the heirloom and traditional native varieties they call "the greatest hits of the gene pool." Handed down through the generations, hardy and refined, these seeds have evolved a natural resistance to drought, disease and pests. They are the "genetic legacy of all the best vegetable seeds cultivated over thousands of years in cultures around the world," quite different from patented hybrids developed and grown commercially, for reasons such as cosmetic appearance, skin touch and shelf life.

Seeds of Change operates a farm in Gila, New Mexico, where they "test grow" seeds people send them from all over the world. Those seeds which are determined marketable are raised by a network of growers all over the United States

One way to preserve Seeds of Change chiles (or any other) is to prepare them in a hot chile oil. You're bound to discover your own ways of using this oil. But, for starters, you might want to: add to softened butter for a piquant spread, then put some on a fresh, crusty split loaf; add garlic puree and run under the broiler for some super-hot garlic bread; sprinkle it on pastas (especially delicious on buckwheat soba noodles); or build a pasta sauce with chile oil, garlic, fresh herbs, ripe olives and grated parmesan; add to a light vinegar for salad dressing; or use it as a mainstay in marinades. Once you start using this condiment, you may wonder how you ever lived without it.

This oil will keep indefinitely. And when the scarlet brew is poured into bottles of interesting shapes and sizes, it makes a superb gift.

Seeds of Change Hot Chile Oil

One cup hot chiles
⅛-½ cup sesame or olive oil

Place fresh chiles and oil in blender. Blend together, strain. Experiment by blending garlic, ginger and/or horseradish to taste.

PESTO NUEVO MEXICO

Sharon Niederman

Be careful when you serve this pesto. It is possible that friends you share it with may beg you for it for years to come. Serve it over fresh pasta, with good Chianti, a salad of mixed baby lettuce, and crisp hot garlic bread, and you may, with a single dinner party, assure your reputation as a chef of formidable power among your set.

Pesto Nuevo Mexico is a svelte combination of native ingredients, prepared with the elan acquired during ten years' dining experience in Northern Italian restaurants. All you need is a blender, the very best ingredients, and a little time. Take a good supply of fresh pinons; abundant, verdant fresh basil, sun-dried tomatoes, excellent olive oil, freshly-grated cheese and Chimayo red chile, and you will surprise yourself.

This pesto is made the way pesto is made in Italy—half parsley and half basil, and it is best made in small batches. Use as a spread on crackers or crostini; if feeling especially indulgent, spread it over a layer of sweet butter. If serving over pasta, add another bit of olive oil and a splash of wine. It's best eaten immediately, while absolutely fresh, because the flavors of the herbs dim and the chile heats up if kept overnight. In the morning, this will not be the same pesto that thrilled your friends the night before.

Pesto Nuevo Mexico

½ cup basil leaves, well-packed
½ cup parsley, well-packed, stems
    removed, Italian if available
⅓ cup fresh, raw pinon (pine) nuts
10-12 slices sun-dried tomato
2-4 teaspoons olive oil
3 tablespoons fresh-grated
    parmesan cheese
1 teaspoon Chimayo red chile,
    finely-ground
3 cloves garlic, chopped
Salt and pepper

Drizzle 1-2 teaspoons of olive oil over the tomatoes. Set aside. In blender or food processor, with 1-2 teaspoons olive oil, pulse first the basil until smooth, then add the parsley leaves and repeat. (You may need to stand by with a spatula and remix the herbs into the blender.) One by one, add and pulse the pinons, garlic, parmesan and red chili. Break the tomatoes into small pieces, add to the mixture. Blend in, getting the pesto as smooth as possible. Don't worry if a few pinons remain whole. Add 1 shake salt and 2 shakes black pepper.